Psychic Protection Made Simple: The Essential Guide

Protect Yourself from Toxic Energies

A Deer Spirit Book

Contents

Introduction 1
What is a Psychic Attack? 6
How Likely Am I to be Psychically Attacked? . 9
Who, or What, Is Likely to be Psychically Attacking You? 13
    Personal Enemies and Rivals 13
    Energy Vampires 13
    Narcissists 15
    Hidden Energies 16
        Thought Forms 17
        Negative Entities 18
        Earthbound Spirits 20
        Black Magic 20
    Don't Ignore the Dark Stuff! 22
How Do I Know I'm Being Psychically Attacked? 24
    Psychic Attack Hits the Aura First 26
Understanding Psychic Energy Helps Prevent Psychic Attack 28
    What is Psychic Energy? 28
    How Does Psychic Energy Work? 29

Everyday Examples That Show How Psychic
Energy Affects Us 30
   Empathy 30
   Intuition 31
   Sensing an Atmosphere 31
   And Some Other Examples You Might Not
   Have Heard About 32
   Psychometry 32

Integrate Your Mind Body and Spirit to Protect Yourself From Psychic Attack 34

What do We Mean by Mind Body and Spirit? 34
   Your Mind 34
   Your Body 35
   Your Spirit 36

Scientific and Spiritual Perspectives 37
   Psychoneuroimmunology (PNI) 37
   The Gut-Brain Axis 38
   Neuroplasticity 38

Integrative Approaches 39

Why Do I Need to Know About the
Interconnectedness of Mind Body and Spirit? 41

Ok, So If It's That Important, Why Don't I
Already Know About it? 42

Authorities, ruling elites and political parties 43
It's the same with the sciences....................44
Religion...44
The media...45

How Do I Tell the Difference Between Positive and Negative Energy? 47

How to Protect Yourself From Psychic Attack 49

The Protective Barrier................................51
How To Do It..52
Clearing and Cleansing 53
External Sources Of Protection; Guides, Angels, the Universe 55
Your Higher Self...56
How to Connect 57
Internal Sources of Psychic Protection 58
How to Strengthen Your Inner Resilience 60
Self-Compassion. 60
Gratitude and Optimism.............................60
A Growth Mindset 63
Connect With Your Inner Wisdom 65
Become More Self-Aware 68

Three Steps Towards Mindful Self Awareness 69
   Observe. 69
   Reflect 70
   Set Boundaries 71
Manage Overwhelm and Accept the Flow of Life 71
   How to Manage Overwhelm 72
   Accept that Life is Full of Ups and Downs.73

Psychic Protection in Popular Culture 76
   Star Wars 79
   Spider-Man 80
   Lord of the Rings 82
   Bram Stoker's Dracula 83
   They Live! 85
   Agatha Christie's Curtain: Poirot's Last Case 86
   Harry Potter and Friends 89

Love: Essential Psychic Protection 92
   Self-Love 92
   Love for Others 93
   Universal Love 94

A Final Word 96

Introduction

Life can be overwhelming. Some days it feels like the world is pressing in on you from all sides.

You're exhausted but can't sleep. Try to stay positive, but negativity slithers in from news, social media, even the people around you. You want peace but conflict seems to follow you around. You do your best to get through the day, but it's as if something invisible is sapping your energy.

Sound familiar?

You're not alone. So many people are realising that they're being affected by energies they can't see and don't fully understand.

If you're an empath, highly sensitive person, or simply someone who feels drained, anxious, or weighed down for no obvious reason, you may be dealing with toxic or disruptive energies. And you need protection.

Psychic protection isn't about superstition or paranoia. It's simply a way of maintaining your emotional, mental and spiritual wellbeing in a world that constantly demands your attention and energy.

Struggling with overwhelming emotions, feeling stuck in negative patterns, or dealing with difficult people who seem to leave you drained? Misfortune, relationship conflicts, or unexplained emotional turmoil, never far away? Feel like you don't belong, that something unseen is holding you back, or that life is harder than it should be, there could be energetic influences at play.

You might feel exhausted no matter how much rest you get, experience chronic anxiety, stress or depression without an obvious cause. Or, like you're struggling against unseen obstacles, or like your thoughts and emotions aren't your own.

In the 21st century, the need for psychic protection has never been greater. We're constantly bombarded with information, opinions, and emotions—online and offline. Social media fills our minds with negativity, fear, and artificial expectations. The news cycle thrives on outrage and division. Technology keeps us connected, but often at the cost of our inner peace. It's not just about avoiding negative people. In today's world, you must manage the sheer volume of energy you're exposed to every single day.

There's a reason for all this. You absorb the energies around you more than you realise. Every interaction, every place you visit, and every piece of media you consume leaves an imprint on your energetic field. If you don't learn how to protect yourself, you can become vulnerable to negativity, manipulation, and energetic drain.

This book isn't about rigid systems, rules, or complicated rituals. It's not another set of beliefs, or instructions to follow. Instead, it's a guide and a collection of practical techniques that you can use in your own way, in your own life.

Each chapter is designed to help you understand different aspects of psychic protection. You'll learn how to shield yourself from draining people and situations, clear negative energy, and maintain your wellbeing in a chaotic world. There's also a chapter on popular culture - how psychic protection is presented in films, books and on TV.

The content is structured to provide both understanding and practical methods to cleanse yourself of negativity and reinforce your energetic resilience. Each practice is easy to incorporate into your routine.

It's useful, if you're an empath or highly sensitive person who tends to take on the emotions and energies of others, you'll learn how to create energetic boundaries so you can interact with the world without becoming drained.

Also, if you work in a healing profession as a therapist, nurse or caregiver, you'll need to be mindful of your energetic wellbeing. It's easy to absorb the pain of others, their stress and their struggles. Here, you'll learn how to avoid burnout, establish strong personal boundaries and protect yourself from unwanted influences. Similarly, if you're just beginning to explore spirituality or are already working with energy—through energy healing, mediumship, or psychic work.

Of course, not everything negative you encounter is the result of an external force. But understanding how to protect yourself from negative energies can be life changing.

Psychic protection isn't just about shielding yourself; it's also about maintaining a strong, positive presence. When your energy is clear and well-protected, you naturally attract more positive experiences. Relationships improve, anxiety subsides, you feel more in control of your life. Grounded and centered, you can navigate life's challenges with confidence and clarity. You'll feel less affected by the world around you,

You no longer need to feel powerless. Nor carry on struggling with exhaustion, anxiety, or negativity. You can take control of your energy and your life. And it starts here.

What is a Psychic Attack?

Bad moods coming out of nowhere? Feeling drained for no good reason? Zest for life diminishing? Sleep paralysis? Periodic personality change? Amnesia? It's possible that you're undergoing psychic attack.

A psychic attack is when a person, group or other entity projects negative energy at another person or group. Psychic attack can be deliberate through focussed intent, ritual, or unconscious – when someone is simply thinking malicious thoughts about another. Often, the intention is to cause harm or distress. Other times, the person projecting negative energy is feeling angry, jealous, resentful or bitter towards another and might not realise they're causing harm.

It happens like this. You're a sovereign being with the ability to control your fate, build your life create your own path, follow your own journey. Sounds good?

The problem is you don't live in a bubble. Instead, you share your world with others, it's an interactive universe. And like the weather, other people can affect you energetically, impact your mood and your decisions. A bit like getting an energetic soaking. Over time, other people's energies can affect your ability to act, think and feel. This is what it's like to be a sovereign being.

When another person cuts you off, slights, snubs or betrays you, it can make you feel bad, deflated, or worst case, like the energy is leaving your body. If this happens a lot, you'll soon feel exhausted and disempowered. If it happens a lot over a long period of time, expect broken relationships, lost jobs, unhappy homes, financial collapse, ill health and lots of other nasty, negative stuff.

Doesn't sound great, and it's not. But don't worry, psychic attack is relatively easy to deal with. If you know it's happening, that is.

The problem is that, often, you won't realise when external energy is affecting you. Imagine walking into a seedy bar, sitting in a traffic jam, or for a positive take on the same process, looking at a beautiful sunset or listening to your favourite song.

You've probably been psychically affected hundreds of times, and don't even know it. What's more, most of the time, neither does the person who's psychically attacking you. Just being annoyed with another person is a form of psychic attack, particularly if you're brooding and feeling malicious. The person might just be in a bad mood, blaming you for something and they don't know their energy is following their thoughts and emotions.

You can also pick up psychic debris from places and people just by being there. Healers and channelers can absorb negative psychic energy while they work. That negativity can stick. Just as positive intent helps people, negativity can blight your life. Imagine collecting someone else's dirty laundry and then wearing some of it under your own clothes for a week.

As mentioned earlier, you can protect yourself against psychic attack. With awareness, positive intent and a few tools, it's possible to lead an authentic, passionate, and purposeful life, even if someone, or something, has got it in for you.

How Likely Am I to be Psychically Attacked?

If you're strong and high vibration, negative psychic energy will more likely bounce directly off your aura. The aura is the energy field that surrounds you. It affects your mental, emotional and physical state. Unfortunately, worry, anger, self-doubt and pessimism all weaken your aura and make you more vulnerable to psychic attack.

Energies are attracted to our specific vibration. Psychic attack is more likely in a low vibration environment where there's a lot of negativity, when you are being driven by subconscious fears and anxieties or if you're too open and trusting, have people-pleasing or blame-shifting tendencies. Similarly, if you are hypnotically suggestible or a psychic and emotional sensitive, you'll be more open to psychic attack. Anything that ends up with you being less in charge of your thoughts and feelings makes you more susceptible to psychic attack.

You're also susceptible if your boundaries are weak or blurred, if you've lost your sense of self or if you lack balance and grounding, or if you haven't processed trauma.

People tend to play certain roles in their family and working lives: scapegoat, enabler, top dog, agony aunt, capable one, poor-me. The problem often comes when someone tries to break out of that role, others, particularly those who have a vested interest in you being seen that way, will look sideways, wonder what's going on. If they have a personal stake in your playing your assigned role, they are likely to react negatively.

You'll more likely be a target for psychic attack if you work or live in a bullying, controlling, environment. Or if it's a place where people see their image all important. In such environments people will be bombarded with negativity, expectation and disapproval.

Empaths, too, are susceptible to psychic attack. Empaths absorb emotions, can form strong connections with others, and as such are prone to energetic overload. Empathy is the capacity to sense and feel another person's feelings and as such, empaths are particularly sensitive to the energies of others around them. This is a good example of psychic connection. But carrying around other people's energy can make empaths susceptible to psychic attack.

Empaths are often trusting and spend a lot of time connecting with others, debating and sharing freely. In doing so, empaths leave themselves open to psychic attack. Even on the internet, empaths are easy prey for narcissists, fantasists and other energy thieves, all of whom aren't slow to send out a few energetic daggers if things don't go their way.

Unresolved karmic patterns are like a magnet for negative energy. Karmic patterns are energy patterns caused by an accumulation of thoughts, words actions and experiences in this lifetime and previous lifetimes, and through generations of your family lineage. Karmic patterns sit in the DNA memory.

DNA memory refers to the idea that certain experiences or traits can be passed down through generations via genetic changes. This explains why karmic patterns are passed down through generations or accumulated over lifetimes. Think of karmic patterns as imprints, which can result in beliefs, behaviours or predispositions that influence your life.

You'll most likely be unaware of karmic patterns, and they can be acknowledged, integrated and healed, and be a positive influence on your life.

However, heavy or unhelpful karmic energies can create an energetic imbalance, disturbance or blockage that can leave you susceptible to psychic attack. Negative people and entities are drawn to these energetic imbalances and will seek to exploit them.

Don't worry, though. You can release energetic imbalances that no longer suit you. There are many talented, experienced past-life experts who will help you do this.

Who, or What, Is Likely to be Psychically Attacking You?

If you understand the motivations and processes behind those predisposed to psychic attack, you can better protect yourself.

Obviously, you can't see a psychic attack, not unless someone is glaring at you from a few feet away. But here's a list of the usual suspects, to help you figure out who the perp is, or might be:

Personal Enemies and Rivals

The most obvious suspects. Someone who has it in for you, who's jealous, harbours resentment, has decided to compete with you at work, in the home, a social setting or online. They might be holding a grudge about something that happened in the past or want something that's yours. If the aggrieved individual can't attack you overtly, or even covertly by undermining you in front of mutual peers, they could resort to psychic attack. It's the only option left for an unempowered person who wants to harm, influence or control you.

Energy Vampires

Ordinary people who feed off the ambient energy of crowds or an individual's benevolent energy. They do this to replenish their own energy and usually have little regard for the consequences of draining yours. In fact, such people will be so focussed on their own needs that they probably won't be aware that there any consequences for you, at all. Being around this type of individual can leave you mentally, emotionally and physically exhausted.

Energy vampires come in various guises. Some behave as control-freaks or egomaniacs. Others like to stir up tensions and instigate conflict. Most of them crave attention, validation and power. Some will moan a lot, focus only on negatives, talk too much, too fast and too often. They might be overly needy and clingy, relying on others to meet their emotional needs. Without psychic protection, energy vampires can even get at you while you're just having a quick chat with them.

Just like the vampires in folklore and popular culture, these individuals will drain your energy leaving you tired and emotionally depleted. If you pass them in the street, they can leave you feeling ungrounded or confused. They can be your passive-aggressive mother who pours on the guilt, or a friend who looks to you to take away his or her pain.

Some energy vampires will try to manipulate you emotionally, guilt trip you, or try to control you, anything to get the energy they need from you. They're predators and to them, you're just sheep in a field.

Remember though, that's just their view of you. You're not a sheep; it's your field, and you can choose who you allow in.

Narcissists

Narcs have many of the same characteristics as an energy vampire, but more besides and this makes them even more dangerous.

They'll psychically attack you to get energy. But they'll also do it to establish control, to secure validation, or just for fun. If things aren't going their way, they'll attack you out of spite, to re-establish control or to punish you.

There are almost as many theories about what a narcissist is and why, as there are actual narcissists. Here, it's enough to say, that these are people who have little or no awareness of where their own personal boundaries start and those of others begin. They'll look at you like you're an inanimate object – say a car, a chair or a bag of crisps. You are only of value during those times they have use for you.

Outside of that you are of no value to them. It's as if you don't actually exist.

In the narcissist's mind, what they want is theirs, already, and if you don't let them have it, they feel aggrieved, denied, insulted and frustrated. Whether or not the thing the narc wants, belongs to them, you, or someone else is to them, of no significance. I want therefore I'm due. Narcissistic entitlement.

Narcissists can psychically attack you when they're in your presence, via social communication technology and through third parties – flying monkeys. Just as in the Wizard of Oz, the witch sent out the winged monkeys to do her bidding, so too does a narcissist surround his or herself with loyal acolytes, eager to attack anyone who falls out of favour with their narcissistic master.

Hidden Energies

So far, we've looked at the normal energetic stuff we pick up from people, albeit troubled or troublesome people. However, other energies exist around us. Hidden energies that are often directed with malign intent, or themselves act with malign intent. Almost always, we're not aware of these energies. These could be Earthbound spirits, negative entities, thought forms.

Just a quick reminder, though. We're not talking about Satan and his demon hordes, here. No need to get out the crucifix and holy water, just yet.

Thought Forms are created by human beings, often without the person knowing it.

As mentioned before, thoughts can shape your reality and if you know how to direct them, they can bring to you the positive things and experiences that match your desires. But what if your thoughts are not positive? What happens when your thoughts don't reflect your desire to have the best for yourself, others and the world?

Thought forms are energetic imprints created by the things you think and feel, your intent and your fears. Most often, they're fleeting, although sometimes, they stick around - say if you're fixated on a particularly intense thought or feeling, for a long time.

Tibetan mysticism says thoughts can become living spiritual beings or material objects. In 1901, Theosophists Annie Beasant and C.W. Leadbeater wrote that thoughts have a radiating vibration and a floating form. The idea that thoughts can manifest as reality is central to Law of Attraction theory.

Thought forms can be helpful allies in helping us manifest our desires. But they can also be sources of limitation, lack and imbalance, attracting negative people and experiences.

Negative Entities We're talking here about beings that originate, it's believed, in non-physical realms such as the astral, or in other dimensions. Unfortunately, these entities can also turn up in your world.

Long ago, entities were conjured up by people who opened doorways into other dimensions. Many are still here, floating around, particularly in old buildings.

Some are powerful and malevolent; others are just low vibrational energies. Demon, jinn, archon, wraith, rakshasa, strigoi – down the years, people have had many different names for such creatures.

When people perform spells, witchcraft, voodoo or manipulate energy, they can, if they're not careful, end up evoking malevolent energies. Often, they do this without realising it. A Ouija board, for instance, can open gateways to different dimensions.

Negative entities hide in the shadows, hoping to infiltrate your consciousness and influence your thoughts, emotions, and behaviours.

They will attack you in a variety of ways. One common trick is to attach themselves to you energetically so they can feed off your energy. In extreme cases, with certain types of entities, this can lead to what religious people call 'possession'.

Again, don't worry too much about entities. We're not talking about the Exorcist films or the Conjuring. You're not going to start foaming at the mouth or see demons flying around the room smashing plates. Most entities are weak and easily removed. The trick is knowing that they're around.

Neither can negative entities physically hurt you – not like in the films. Instead, they manipulate your thoughts, emotions and perceptions with intrusive statements that can undermine your feelings about yourself, your life, the world around you, and set you against others. Fear, unease, dread, anxiety, a sense of being persecuted – these are the tools of an entity's trade. Unhelpful thoughts implanted by entities, act as triggers, sparking off negative behaviour patterns. Or they might just by interfere with your energy body creating weaknesses that make you more susceptible to influence.

Earthbound Spirits are energy forms containing aspects of a dead person's consciousness, trapped on the Earth plane. They are either attracted to the energy of a person or of a place. Some are helpful, offering guidance and support; others can pose a threat to our energetic wellbeing.

A spirit is piece of functioning consciousness, in that it has its own identity. But it's also tied up with your identity. You're more likely to encounter a threatening spirit if you have a low vibrational frequency, an energy imbalance or if you're carrying around a lot of negative energy or karma.

Spirits, like humans, have their own consciousness and make choices about what they do and don't do. A spirit with unresolved trauma or unfulfilled desires is more likely to try and inveigle its way into your energy body looking for solace or energy. Like entities, spirits feed off energy, can severely weaken you and make you do, think and feel things differently than you otherwise would.

Black Magic. Put simply, black magic is the use of manipulative occult and esoteric practices for malevolent purposes, sent with harmful intent. And yes, there are people out there who practice it. People who deliberately manipulate energy use rituals, hexes, spells, curses, summon up entities and spirits, draw upon negative energies.

Black magicians might do this for several reasons. Most obviously out of jealousy or to get what they want from you. Some will attack you psychically because they think you've upset them, or to settle scores with perceived enemies and rivals. They might send black magic, hoping to control or weaken you or to get the upper hand in a conflict. Sometimes they do it for the sheer hell of it – because that's just the kind of person that they are.

The aim of a black magic psychic attack is to cause the target psychological and emotional distress, to induce fear or disrupt your life. You're more susceptible to it if you and those around you, believe in the power of magic, if you're easily suggestible to influence and exploitation.

Each person who sends black magic to others will probably have their own methods and practices. But in general, it's about focussing harmful or negative intent at a target. The negative energy sent is believed to get into the target's mind and aura

Some black magicians use photos, online profiles or personal items (if they have them) to create a stronger connection with their target. They can even use a hair or DNA sample, so watch out who you let loose in your bathroom.

To send their attacks, black magicians use chanting, negative affirmations, symbols, curses. Some might visualise or draw the harms they wish to cause or stick pins or knives into a physical representation of their target, say a voodoo doll. Others create thought forms, energetic constructs that can attach to their chosen target.

A black magic psychic attack could manifest as bad luck, anxiety, disruption, feelings of vulnerability. Over time, it can have a devastating effect on your mental health and wellbeing.

Don't Ignore the Dark Stuff!

It's an interactive universe and not everything in it exudes love and light. In such a place, it's vital that you learn how to protect yourself from these energies. Our mental and emotional and spiritual wellbeing depends on it.

You might prefer to ignore the dark stuff, think only of positive, good and light. You might even refuse to perceive that negativity exists, or if it does that it doesn't exist in your world. Whatever you do, don't make it your own personal Voldemort, that which cannot be spoken of.

Blissful ignorance isn't helpful. However much you refuse to acknowledge its relevance to your life and however much you want your world to be about love and light, when dealing with universal energy and mixing with other sentient beings, you need to be aware that energy can be harnessed for both good and bad purposes.

None of that means you're a jelly, though. Remember that you have a few powers of you own - clarity, resilience, awareness, intention. And knowledge. Study the dark stuff, get to understand it, then you can protect yourself from it. With some knowledge and your own power, you can safeguard yourself from harm and maintain your energetic sovereignty.

How Do I Know I'm Being Psychically Attacked?

Psychic attacks will show themselves, if you know what you're looking for. To protect yourself, it's important to recognise the signs and symptoms. For instance:

- Sudden exhaustion, chronic headaches with no identifiable medical reason.

- Unexplained intense emotional shift, without any obvious external trigger.

- Insomnia, nightmares, restless sleep, exhausted on waking.

- Irritability or mood swings.

- Depression, feeling unusually sad or hopeless.

- Difficulty concentrating, focussing or making decisions.

- Intrusive, disturbing negative thoughts about yourself or others that linger and spiral out of control.

- Unexplained aches and pains, often in the neck or shoulders.

- Feeling emotionally and physically drained.

- Feeling paranoid, persecuted, anxious, not wanting to gout and mix with people
- Heaviness or blockages in your energy field.
- Self-doubt, apathy, forgetfulness and confusion.

These signs are also symptoms of many other phenomena – mental, physical, emotional, spiritual – and don't necessarily indicate a psychic attack. Check out your mental health first, just in case there is a medical issue you need to be aware of.

If you suffer a repeat energetic attack, it can sit in your energy fields and invite similar experiences. Certain people can pick up on the energy, usually the types who need that energy. These characters work out that you are vulnerable or keen to help and take advantage.

If you carry this sort of psychic debris around long enough, it can alter your belief system and self-image. It's how advertising works: "I'll feel better if I do this," you might think. But what's actually happening is the opposite: "This is what someone else wants me to do, so if I do it, at least I won't get any more grief." Or in other words, if I do what the other wants me to do, the bombardment of negative energy will stop.

Psychic Attack Hits the Aura First

Imagine a solar flare hitting the Earth's electro-magnetic field. The aura is a subtle but vital energetic field which surrounds all life forms. It has seven layers powered by seven major chakras, rotating cones or spiral vortices of energy. It connects us with everything but also allows us to be discrete individuals. Your thoughts and feelings directly affect it - depression, exhaustion, illness, disease and accidents are all a reflection of the health of your aura.

Your aura is a living, pulsating field which you can draw in to within an inch of your body or extend outward, infinitely, A strong aura means a strong spiritual connection, physical health and mental and emotional stability.

If you're strong and high vibration, negativity will bounce directly off your aura. However, a psychic attack can disrupt your aura, creating vulnerabilities. It's then that negative energy can get into your system and affect your physical, mental and emotional state.

Psychic protection isn't just about learning how to ward off negative influences, though. It's also about understanding how psychic energy works. When you have this understanding, you become more resilient to the influences around you and more able to deal with life's challenges.

Understanding Psychic Energy Helps Prevent Psychic Attack

What is Psychic Energy?

Psychic energy is a subtle force that connects the universe and everything in it, people included. It's what ties together the structure of reality. It flows through all living beings and connects us to each other.

In psychology and certain spiritual traditions, it's a non-physical force that influences mental and emotional processes. Philosopher and psychologist, Carl Jung, claimed it was the energy derived from unconscious drives, thoughts, and emotions that fuel mental activities and behaviour. In modern spiritual thought, psychic energy is often associated with the aura and chakras.

If we could see it, psychic energy would most likely appear to us in various shapes and frequencies. We know it's there because it affects our feelings views, beliefs, emotions and ideas, and as a result, it can shape our life experiences. Higher frequencies align with positive emotions like love, joy, and gratitude, whereas negative emotions - fear, anger, and resentment - vibrate at lower frequencies.

How Does Psychic Energy Work?

To protect yourself psychically you need to understand how psychic energy works. Everything is energy and everything gives off energy. Wherever you go you're surrounded by the stuff, whether you're aware of it or not. A lot of energy is positive, often its negative.

You might think that you're a discrete, separate individual, but you live in an interactive world that is divergent and competitive. Where peoples' desires, needs and interests are not always in alignment with harmony. Being sovereign doesn't mean you are unaffected by what's going on around you.

Once we realise that psychic energy exists, we can start to see how everything is interrelated in a world where the invisible affects the visible. Psychic energy responds to intention and focus. It's how psychics and mediums work and how healers direct energy.

Your thoughts and emotions release electromagnetic vibrations that resonate with comparable frequencies in the cosmic field, much like a magnet pulls iron filings. Your frequency affects your emotional state, and your emotional state reflects your frequency. The universe is a vast electro-magnetic field which receives your thought and emotion and sends you proportionate experiences.

The Law of Attraction, as described by Esther Hicks, is a philosophy, that suggests we can focus our thoughts and intentions to create the life we want. Law of Attraction advocates believe that positive or negative thoughts and feelings bring you positive or negative experiences into your life. Positive energy attracts success in health, finances, relationships. To attract those things into your life all you have to do is focus on whatever your heart desires - visualise goals, positive mindset and believe that desired outcomes are achievable. This, they say, is because thoughts are also energy.

Everyday Examples That Show How Psychic Energy Affects Us

Empathy. You're taking to a friend who is feeling sad. Before they even tell you, what's going on with them, you can already sense their emotional state. This is psychic energy at work through empathy. You are picking up on your friend's emotional vibrations. This energy exchange helps you to better understand and support your friend and creates a deeper emotional connection.

Intuition. You're about to buy a new house, accept a job offer, make some other important decision. Everything seems ok, going to plan. But you have an uncomfortable gut feeling, nagging away at you.

This is your intuition telling you that something isn't right. This is our inner guidance system that connect us with our subconscious and that picks up cues from our surroundings that we're not consciously aware of.

If you listen to messages like this, further investigation may throw up new or hidden information that might get you to rethink your course of action.

Sensing an Atmosphere. You walk into a room where people have just been arguing. The verbal exchanges have stopped but the atmosphere is still tense and heavy. How can you feel this? Because the psychic energy from the intense emotions linger in the space, affecting your own energy field.

Even if the people involved have left the room and there's no visible sign of conflict, you might still feel a heavy, tense atmosphere. Your own energy body picks this up and interprets the psychic imprint left over by the previous conflict. It's the same reason that we feel uplifted and energised when entering a place filled with positive energy, where people are celebrating, meditating or happy, say a festival, a children's birthday party or a mind body spirit show.

So, don't forget - psychic energy flows between people and environments, influencing feelings, thoughts, and behaviour.

And Some Other Examples You Might Not Have Heard About

Psychometry is the ability to sense or read the history of an object by touching it. Suppose you pick up an old, antique ring at a flea market. As you hold it, you start to receive images, emotions, or impressions about its previous owner. You might even see glimpses of their life or feel their emotions.

Psychometry is based on the belief that objects can absorb and retain the energy of people who have interacted with them. Some individuals, it is believed, can tap into this retained energy to glean information about the past.

Telepathic Animal Communication. A pet owner might sense that their dog is feeling unwell or distressed without the dog showing obvious signs of illness. An encounter with a deer or a hawk might be seen as a message from spirit, with the animal crossing your path because there is something you need to know.

The belief goes that thoughts, emotions, or images are transmitted between human and animal. You understand the animal's needs and feelings more deeply and receive impressions about their condition or desires.

Remote Viewing. A remote viewer believes that they can see a distant or unseen target, without being there themselves. They usually do this through extrasensory perception (ESP). Through meditation or focussed concentration, the remote viewer sees inside their head, details of the place, maybe the layout of the rooms, specific objects, or even what's happening. Using psychic energy in this way, the remote viewer gathers information without being physically present.

Integrate Your Mind Body and Spirit to Protect Yourself From Psychic Attack

When you understand how psychic energy works you start to become aware of the flow of mental and spiritual forces around you. You'll know better how these forces influence your thoughts, emotions, and wellbeing. And as you become more adept at spotting when you've picked something up, or if something external is getting at you; you'll know when to put up psychic defences or strengthen your energy fields.

You'll be more resilient against psychic attack and other pernicious influences. The quickest way to do all this? Integrate your mind, body and spirit, of course. And strengthen your mindset.

What do We Mean by Mind Body and Spirit?

Your Mind is your awareness and intelligence centre. It encompasses your cognitive processes, ideas, convictions, thoughts and senses and allows you to access your consciousness, form attitudes and worldviews, learn things, solve problems and engage in self-reflection. Reason, logic, and creativity all sit within the mind. Know your own mind and you'll more likely be able to tell if something external is influencing your thoughts.

When your mental state is positive it can help your body stay healthy and you spirit more vibrant. Poor mental health can affect our physical health, leading to hypertension, ulcers and many other physical conditions. Poor mental health can also affect you spiritually, evoking feelings of emptiness or despair. It's in states such as this, where you're most susceptible to psychic attack.

Your Body is where you feel the richness of life. It encompasses your physiological processes, physical abilities, and your sensory impressions. It's what enables you to express yourself and engage with the outside world.

Humans have three main intelligence senses - the brain-mind complex, heart centre and gut centre. One or all three of these will be triggered if something isn't quite right around you.

Good physical health helps maintain the mind and spirit. Get good nutrition, regular exercise and enough good quality sleep and you'll have mental clarity and emotional stability, which in turn can lead to a more harmonious spiritual life.

A classic sign of psychic attack is when you unexpectedly lose the desire to exercise or suddenly feel too exhausted to workout. This is particularly debilitating because it's the oxygen moving around the body and the accompanying muscle movements which repel a lot of unwanted, negative energy.

When you're ill or injured you tend to focus on your immediate physical health and its harder to think positively or concern yourself with much else. Remember the last time you had a toothache, a bad back, or a hangover?

Being ill or injured is often the body's way of telling you to stop or slow down. This is especially the case in long-term psychic attack because the body's systems suffer. Your body is asking you to wake up, get some clarity and take action to stop whoever or whatever is attacking. When you do slow down and have no option but to rest. Then you have time to relax, introspect, walk with nature, read, meditate.

Your Spirit exists outside of space and time and represents the core of who you really are, your deeper sense of purpose and an innate sense of connection to something greater than yourself.

From your spirit, you receive guidance on your path to self-discovery and spiritual awakening. It's the source of your inner wisdom, intuition and encompasses your values, beliefs, and sense of meaning. Your spirit also contains your love and empathy. Listen to it for peace, harmony and fulfilment. If you let it, your spirit will help you play your part in bringing the universe, everyone and everything it, together.

A healthy spirit can provide comfort, resilience and a sense of hope – both crucial in protecting yourself from psychic interference. However, spiritual crises can manifest as mental distress or even physical ailments. And it's when you're at you lowest ebb that you'll be more likely to pick up external stuff that you'd rather not have around.

Scientific and Spiritual Perspectives

Scientific Research and Spiritual Belief Offer Insights on the Interconnectedness Of Mind Body and Spirit

Psychoneuroimmunology (PNI) is a field of science that explores the interaction between psychological processes, the nervous system, and the immune system. Research in PNI demonstrates that stress and emotional states can significantly impact physical health. For example, chronic stress can suppress immune function making the body more susceptible to illnesses. PNI research also shows that positive emotional states - happiness and contentment - can enhance immune function and overall health.

The Gut-Brain Axis links the emotional and cognitive centres of the brain with peripheral intestinal functions. The gut microbiota, the community of microorganisms living in the digestive tract, plays a crucial role in this communication. Imbalances in gut microbiota have been linked to mental health disorders such as anxiety and depression.

Neuroplasticity is the brain's ability to reorganise itself by forming new neural connections. Practices such as mindfulness meditation and physical exercise have been shown to enhance neuroplasticity, thus improving mental health and cognitive function.

Ancient Traditions such as Ayurveda, Traditional Chinese Medicine and many indigenous healing practices, emphasise mind body spirit balance and harmony for optimal health. Each recommends practices, dietary guidelines and spiritual rituals to maintain this balance.

Yoga, tai chi, and qigong are based on the belief that physical, mental, and spiritual well-being is interconnected and can be developed simultaneously. Yoga, for example, combines physical postures (asanas), breath control (pranayama), and meditation (dhyana) to promote holistic health.

Native American tradition has long used rituals, ceremonies and holistic healing to maintain mind body spirit balance. They do this through connection to traditions and nature. Ceremonies, for instance sweat lodges and sun dances, promote physical purification and spiritual renewal. Herbs, rituals, and storytelling are integrated into healing practices to promote inner harmony and connection with the land. Rituals reinforce a sense of community, identity, and reverence for the interconnectedness of all living beings, past, present and future.

Integrative Approaches

Addressing the physical, mental, and spiritual dimensions of health can lead to more comprehensive and effective care, it is believed. The body-mind complex is a holistic system. If one part of that system fails to work properly, the complex will compensate in other parts. This, however, can create an imbalance in the whole system, which is why the dysfunctional aspect needs to be rectified.

Integrative medicine blends conventional medical treatments with evidence-based alternative therapies such as acupuncture, chiropractic and nutrition therapy to treat the whole person.

Ayurveda, the traditional Indian system of medicine has long advocated that people do yoga and meditation to connect their mind, body, spirit.

According to traditional Chinese medicine, the flow of vital energy (or Qi) through the body's meridians, is crucial to diagnosing and treating illness. There are twelve primary meridians, each associated with a specific organ system, which enable Qi and blood to circulate around the body. Techniques like acupuncture and acupressure target specific points along the meridians, to ensure the smooth flow of Qi.

Interconnectedness is also central to many modern holistic health practices and belief systems. For instance, mindfulness-based stress reduction combines meditation and yoga to improve mental and physical well-being. Naturopaths use natural remedies, lifestyle counselling and nutritional support to promote self-healing and balance.

Why Do I Need to Know About the Interconnectedness of Mind Body and Spirit?

Your mind body and spirit really are connected. Each aspect supports and sustains the others. So, understanding and nurturing this interconnectedness can lead to a more balanced and fulfilling life. By integrating your mental, physical and spiritual self you can achieve a more harmonious and resilient existence. This in turn, will leave you less susceptible to psychic attack.

You'll more easily recognise the flow of mental and spiritual forces that influence our thoughts, emotions, and wellbeing. With this awareness you can more easily identify when you're being attacked. You'll know when to strengthen your energy fields against negative influences learn to be more mindful of your emotional and psychological boundaries.

Both ancient and modern beliefs suggest that the three elements are deeply interwoven, each influencing and reflecting, the state of the others. Mind body, spirit balance is essential for overall wellness. When you have it, you're a lot less prone to psychic attack.

Why? Because you are happy, on-path, so you don't seek out trouble or want to ward off danger.

You don't take dangerous risks or seek thrills, you don't attract negative people who hurt you, your sunny disposition is unwavering. In this state, you refuse to accept anything less than your heart's desire, you trust the universe, yourself and others. You are also calm and peaceful, a frequency the body loves.

Ok, So If It's That Important, Why Don't I Already Know About it?

You probably haven't read Douglas Adams's "Dirk Gently" novels or seen the TV shows. Gently is a self-professed holistic detective who believes that the universe is a complex, interwoven system where everything affects everything else. To his mind, minor, seemingly trivial occurrences can have significant impacts on larger events. Like the 'butterfly effect', apparently unrelated events, people, and objects can be deeply interconnected. Understanding these connections is crucial to uncovering the truth, Adams has Gently believe.

Gently however, lives in a dirty little office and deals with seemingly insignificant little cases and can only dream of a life of languid luxury in the sun. Everyone thinks he's a waster, and that his ideas and beliefs belong to the lunatic fringe.

Through Dirk Gently, Douglas Adams provides a clear message from mainstream society. Believe in this stuff and you're delusional and you'll fail. But while we're talking about fictional characters, remember what Captain America once said in the Marvel comics. This was at a time when he was fighting against corporate interests, the government, Iron Man and his former friends, and when public opinion was against him for the first time.

"Even if everyone is telling you that something wrong is something right. Even if the whole world is telling you to move, it is your duty to plant yourself like a tree, look them in the eye, and say, No, *you* move'".

We live in a world where culture, science, religion, the authorities and the media emphasise and reinforce division, compartmentalisation and separation. It's a dog-eat-dog world, we're constantly told, a world where there is never enough. Not enough money, time, stuff, safety, security, success and anything else that anyone might want or need.

Authorities, ruling elites and political parties of all persuasion emphasise distinctions between social classes. The resulting economic and social segregation harms societal cohesion and because of this, people form identities based on their social and economic status, distancing themselves from others who they perceive to have different social and economic standing, and sometimes, racial differences. Seeing people in terms of how they are different to you, institutionalises separation, encourages discrimination and creates even greater social inequality.

It's the same with the sciences. Biology, chemistry, and physics are often studied in isolation, for academic reasons. People are taught to view each science in terms of separate content rather than common processes that would help people better understand the world.

Religion, supposedly the antithesis of science, follows the same separatist, divisive patterns. Monty Python had it in their 1979 satirical film, Life of Brian. Who shall we join to fight off the Roman invaders- Judean People's Front or the People's Front of Judea? What shall we follow to reach the Kingdom of Heaven - the Gourd or the Shoe? Religious leaders emphasise distinctions between believers and non-believers. Or between their followers and followers of another religion? Follow me and you'll go to Heaven! Don't follow me and you're off to see the big red guy with the fiery breath and the big pointy trident. Too often, what follows, is a sense of exclusivity, division, intolerance and conflict.

The media, too, tends to highlight differences rather than commonalities. Outrage, sensationalism and conflict sells papers and encourages internet clicks. It also satisfies the personal political-economic agendas of rich billionaire owners and their investor buddies. And glorifies celebrities, encouraging you to aspire to their status, but never achieve it

What you get as a consumer is usually a lot of manipulative rubbish designed to amplify perceived separations between groups, political parties, cultural communities. Polarised society, it seems, is better for business than the interconnectedness of human experience. No wonder Dirk Gently never made much money in the Douglas Adams books.

Living in a world full of separation, conflict, dysfunction, and division, makes it harder for you to defend yourself against psychic attack. There's so much negativity flying around that it can be hard to even to recognise when you're being attacked.

In such a fragmented society you're regularly experiencing negative emotions - fear, anger, isolation, loss, grief. This can weaken your mental state and erode your energetic defences, making it easier for harmful psychic influences to affect you. As can a collective atmosphere of distrust and hostility.

If your energy fields are compromised, you'll be less able to detect and deflect negative influences. However, when you integrate your mind body and spirit, you create inner strength and harmony, and greater resilience.

This helps you critically assess and negative, divisive messages – wherever they come from – and resist societal and peer, pressures.

With greater self-awareness, emotional stability and mental clarity, you'll be able to remain grounded when there's negativity around. You'll also be able to retain your focus, whether that's on unity, compassion, love, or even your favourite computer game, book or TV show.

A word of warning about what you do watch, read or listen to, long-term. Your brain isn't greatly different to your computer when it's processing data. Rubbish in, rubbish out. But not only that. If you store too much insignificant rubbish in your brain, there's less space for the important stuff.

How Do I Tell the Difference Between Positive and Negative Energy?

As mentioned earlier, energy is the invisible force that enlivens the universe. It flows through all living beings and through their consciousness, helps shape the fabric of reality.

Energy is neutral, it becomes positive or negative through consciousness

Humans, animals, entities and whatever else the universe has created, impress their desires, fears, thoughts, feelings and actions onto the universe's energetic field.

When you entrain your consciousness onto the field, you create experiences. This is why what you feel and think about yourself is reflected in your life, the lessons you need to learn, your weaknesses and contradictions.

You might bump into someone you need to speak to today without realising you actually created that meeting. A book will fall from a shelf in the library, the very book that you need right now. It's not the universe doing that, it's your own consciousness speaking to the universe and asking it to deliver.

When interacting with consciousness, energy can be uplifting and nourishing, draining and discordant, bland and neutral. When you encounter positive energy you'll feel love, joy, compassion, and harmony. You can recognise it in moments of profound joy, beauty or inspiration. Positive energy uplifts and inspires, infuses your life with vitality, creativity and connection. You feel supported and aligned with your highest potential.

If there's negative energy around, however, that won't feel so great. Fear, anger, resentment, discord - take your pick. Negative energy drains and depletes. You'll feel heavy, tense, disconnected, stressed, anxious, annoyed, the list goes on. Sometimes the effect will be more subtle. You might just feel a bit off, agitated or distracted, out of alignment with yourself and the world around you.

How to Protect Yourself From Psychic Attack

The aim here is to try and help you understand the energetic patterns that influence your experiences. That way you can develop a better awareness of your emotional landscape. From this awareness, you'll know when, how and why, you sometimes need to take action to protect yourself.

There are many ways you can protect yourself psychically, many practices that you can learn, many sources of help you can access. Some involve working with your inner self, some with external sources. All can be tailored to your individual needs and circumstances.

Psychic protection intersects with many aspects of mental, emotional and spiritual life. People have different beliefs, experiences, cultural backgrounds, energetic needs, unique sensitivities and fears. Approaches to psychic protection reflect the broad spectrum of human experience and the different ways people find balance and peace.

The types of energies one person encounters may be different than for another. Some people are more sensitive to energies and therefore more vulnerable to emotional mental or spiritual disturbances. People who face a lot of stress at work or in their relationship might need a different approach to somebody who is struggling with episodes from their past. One person might need to enhance their inner strength and resilience, while another might draw comfort and security from external rituals or spiritual practises.

There's one important thing to remember, here. Don't be swayed by fast-talking gurus and any unique, exclusive, approach to psychic protection that they might be peddling.

When someone tells you that you can only do something only one way, it usually tells you more about the intent of the person who is promoting the approach. And not much about whether the advice is useful to you – which is, you know, the only actual point of advice.

One-way usually means their-way, which itself, is a sort of psychic attack, as the guru seeks to override your own thoughts, feelings and instincts with their dogma. Unfortunately, such people can be very convincing. They can come on very strong if you disagree with them and threaten all kinds of negative consequences if you don't do as they say.

The Levellers, a rock band from the UK, dear to my heart, had it. 'There's Only One Way; And that's Your Own.' So, use your intuition and your critical thinking brain to choose the approach to psychic protection that you feel is right for you, given your personal circumstances and particular needs. What areas of your life is negativity creeping into? Where and how do you feel vulnerable?

Take in the information below, introspect, experiment with different methods an see how each affects your wellbeing. Your psychic wellbeing is unique to you, and so too should be the methods you use to protect it.

The Protective Barrier

Creating a protective barrier around your energy field helps keep you balanced, clear and resilient. It fortifies your energetic boundaries and separates your personal energy field from external influences. This stops harmful and unwanted energies from penetrating your energy field.

Protective barriers define your personal space and establish your control over what belongs to you. This type of protection also enables you to filter out negative energies you're carrying around and keeps any new negativity at a healthy distance. In this way, you maintain your sense of self, inner harmony and balance. You block the other's vibration just as an umbrella stops the rain or armour might protect against physical weapons.

How To Do It

- Visualise the protection forming around you – armour, umbrella, bubble, cocoon – whatever you feel safe with.
- Affirm that with this protection, you are safe and will experience no harm. And that only love, peace and positive energy can get in.
- Crystals such as tourmaline, orgone, shungite, obsidian or amethyst can help strengthen your protective shield. Rituals, prayers, or meditation can help you create a safe space for yourself.
- Ground your energy to create a connection to the Earth which dispels excess and unwanted energy.

These techniques are useful when entering a challenging or energetically charged environment. Before you go to the potentially difficult place or meeting set your intention to reinforce your energetic boundaries. Energies can be more intense in large crowds particularly when people are already in an emotional state, say a demonstration, sports match or music concert.

Such environments can be overwhelming, particularly if you're sensitive to others' energies. With so many people around, each with their own unique energies, you can quickly feel anxious, stressed, emotionally exhausted or drained. When you're in such a heightened emotional state, it can be easy to attract negativity to yourself without even realising it.

Your protective shield will help you in challenging situations and environments. So too will deep breathing exercises, which can help calm your nervous system and restore balance to your energy field.

Clearing and Cleansing

We're all used to the idea of maintaining good physical hygiene – showering, washing our hands, cleaning our teeth, having a nice massage or a haircut, soaking in a hot bath.

It's just as important to do all of this for your energetic hygiene. Good energetic hygiene helps prevent you from accumulating negative, harmful energies that will make you vulnerable to psychic attack. If these unwanted energies are left unchecked, they can weaken your energetic boundaries allowing psychic intrusions to penetrate your defences.

A strong vibrant energy field is a natural barrier against psychic attacks. If your energy is robust, you become more resilient to external pressures and less likely to absorb emotions and thoughts from others. You are more attuned to subtle shifts in your environment and your own consciousness and can quickly identify when something doesn't feel right.

Energetic hygiene involves caring for your aura chakras and meridians. Practising energetic care regularly, you can release stagnant energy, clear away negativity and support the free flow of energy throughout your system. It's no different to removing dirt toxin impurities from your physical body. Establish a daily routine and you'll feel more peaceful balanced, harmonious and be able to embrace life with more clarity and vitality.

- Start with a morning meditation to centre yourself and set a positive intent for the day.
- Use energy clearing techniques at set, specific times to help cleanse and purify your energy field. Use crystals, sage, incense, singing balls and tuning forks.

Target them on areas where you feel tension, heaviness or anxiety.
- Breathwork or gentle movement practises like Tai Chi or yoga can reduce tension and stimulate energy flow in your body.
- Ground yourself by spending time in nature. This can revitalise your energy and queue into the present moment.
- Whilst showering, visualise negative energies washing way and imagine the water as a cleansing, healing force.
- In the evening, take a moment to reflect on your day and prepare for a restful night's sleep. You can use a journal to write things down. Or if you prefer, just sit quietly and release tension and worries from the day.

Incorporating practises like these into your daily routine enables you to clean, balance and recharge your energy field.

External Sources Of Protection; Guides, Angels, the Universe

You'll find a lot of guidance, wisdom and knowledge available about where to go for protection. Depending on what you believe in, you can develop a relationship with your angels, spirit or animal guides, ascended masters, your ancestors or other divine beings.

All these sources of help (well call them 'your guides' for reasons of brevity) can assist you in challenging times and help guide you towards safety and wellbeing. They offer comfort reassurance and strength and can help you stay grounded and centred when life gets difficult. Your guides can also help you overcome obstacles. release limiting beliefs, past traumas and, of course, help you deal with and prevent, psychic attack.

Your Higher Self

This is your eternal aspect, the most authentic, wise and spiritually connected aspect of who you are. It's the part of you that transcends ego and everyday material and social concerns. It gives you a broader perspective based on wisdom compassion and a deep understanding of your soul's journey, your true purpose, the greater good and the pursuit of the truth. Your higher self is connected to the Universal consciousness and provides you with guidance that aligns to your highest potential.

Assistance from your guides or your higher self will most likely come in the form of something positive, helpful or useful, rather than a message or sudden thought that is negative or judgmental (this is more likely a sign of a psychic attack) Maybe a gut feeling, a flash of inspiration, an impression or synchronicity.

Connect with your guides and your higher self and you can better make decisions that align with your highest good. As a result, you'll more likely avoid conflicts.

How to Connect

- Create moments of stillness where you can focus on the connection and open your mind and heart to receive guidance and insight.
- Trust your intuition and pay attention to subtle cues gut feelings that may indicate the presence of guidance.
- Listen carefully and be open to receiving guidance in unexpected ways, say through dreams, visions, synchronicities.
- Use rituals to state your intentions, offer gratitude and to invite guidance and protection into your life. You might want to create a special space where you do this. This could be a physical space like a room, or it could be a mental space, for instance a

safe haven that you have created through visualisation.
- Reiki and other energy medicine practices can help. You channel pure, love energy which aims to balance and release negativity, even from the cells of the body. When you love and accept who you are, understand your place in a benevolent universe and believe that you are a master of your own destiny, it's almost impossible for a third party to undermine you. This is true power. More on love, later.

Internal Sources of Psychic Protection

To protect yourself psychically, you need to focus on the externals, such as places, people and things, where the attacks are coming from, but also on your own internal makeup. In fact, it could be your own internal makeup that attracted the negative experience. Maybe you haven't honoured yourself, misunderstood what is going on or not taken care of things you should have taken care of. A shaky, wobbly sense of things being out of control is a sign of a psychic attack, but also an invitation to be, psychically attacked.

Life can be uncertain and full of challenges. When things don't how you want, it's easy to get overwhelmed with worries, anxiety, fears and give in to negative thoughts. These unhealthy thoughts could be about yourself, the people you know, the world around you, your future, and the universe. At times like this you are particularly susceptible to psychic attack. It's essential therefore to build inner resilience in order to deal with adversity.

With inner resilience you can bounce back from setbacks and hardship. You can adapt to change, remain grounded and centred in the face of challenges, be flexible in how you adapt to change, remain optimistic and hopeful in difficult times. You might even learn to thrive in adversity and use difficult experiences to develop confidence and capacity to cope better with your life and the world around you.

We're not suggesting here that you avoid challenges or deny adverse situations. However, if you develop inner resilience, you can face adversity with courage, confidence and determination.

When you know there is a reason you came here, that you are going to feel this way often because of the nature of the world and the way it is run, by those in power. When you have this realisation, it is easier to accept that things will never be perfect and that however strong you become, unexpected things are likely to affect you. It's your reaction that's important. Will you respond by loving who you are? Or compromising yourself? Will you give too much and not take enough?

How to Strengthen Your Inner Resilience

Self-Compassion. Treat yourself with kindness and compassion during difficult times. Psychic attacks get into your weak spots and prompt you into focusing on what you think is wrong with you. This evokes negative self-talk and belief – 'I'm not enough, unlikeable, unlovable, selfish, a failure' – all that sort of thing.

Give yourself a break, realise that everyone has weak points and handles some things better than others. Practice self-care rituals – meditation or journaling - spend time in nature to relax, ground and nurture yourself. Remind yourself that asking for help isn't a sign of weakness and that everyone needs time to rest and recharge. Sometimes you just have to take a step back and take some time for yourself. Do what you need, regardless of what anyone else thinks.

Gratitude and Optimism. It can be easy to look at what's wrong rather than what's right. Or what you don't like rather than what you do like. Particularly when things are not going well.

Unfortunately, a pessimistic outlook makes you more susceptible to psychic attack. It amplifies your vulnerability to external influences and diminishes your natural energetic defences.

If you always expect the worst to happen then you can Inadvertently attract and manifest negative outcomes – bad luck, accidents, toxic relationships.

This sort of thinking, when cyclical, can become a self-fulfilling prophecy where you unintentionally invite negative energy into your life. Preoccupation with thoughts like this can also lower your defences. Particularly if you are already in a state of mental and emotional distress, feel powerless, lack confidence or have weak personal boundaries.

So, for instance, if you feel undervalued in general or that you are constantly being criticised; you are likely to be more affected by criticism, real or perceived. A pessimistic mindset can also attract the type of people and who thrive on exploiting fear, doubt and insecurity.

If you often feel like this, down on yourself, chances are it could have come from your childhood. It is natural and normal for you to feel happy, go with the flow, plan when you can and relax about life in general. But if your childhood was difficult, say you didn't get the love, care and support you needed, or worse still, you were abused or neglected, you are likely to feel uptight, fearful, and be wary of what might happen; always prepared, just in case.

If you carry fears around with you, you can become a target for toxic people. You are giving off emotional vulnerability and they are drawn to this. When you're vulnerable, toxic people know their manipulative tactics will be more effective and they will be more able to control and dominate you.

The toxic person might, for instance, capitalise on your fear of abandonment by isolating you from family and friends so you become more dependent on your relationship with them. If you doubt your abilities, the toxic person might bully you into accepting unfair treatment, as you feel that you have no other options.

In such cases, a pessimistic outlook enables toxic individuals to capitalise on your insecurities and reinforce your negative self-beliefs. Fear, anger and despair lower your personal energy vibration On the other hand, positive emotions like love, gratitude, and optimism can raise your energy vibration, which helps create the protective barrier mentioned earlier.

A Growth Mindset. See challenges, not as obstacles to be avoided, but opportunities for growth and learning.

Say you are getting consistent harsh criticism from a colleague, a boss or a family member. Or you're dealing with a person who uses manipulative tactics or emotional intimidation to undermine your confidence.

Both cases can be seen as a psychic attack as, over time, their actions start to erode your self-esteem and mental wellbeing. Particularly if the criticism or intimidation negatively affects your life in some way, say you lose friends, miss a promotion, or you're excluded from a family event.

In all these cases, to begin with you may feel overwhelmed and disheartened. You might think that the criticism means that you're inadequate, or that the challenge is too great to overcome.

However, you can overcome challenges and adapt to new situations. You do this by developing new abilities, greater emotional intelligence and by building defences against the emotional impact of the criticism and the challenging situation.

To do this, first analyse what went wrong, then gather information about the situation. From this, you can identify areas for improvement or where to look for guidance. See setbacks as temporary and opportunities for development. Focus on what you can control and take proactive steps towards your objective.

Take this line and you can work out what went wrong and use the new knowledge to refine your future approach.

Face challenging moments with a willingness to understand and improve. You might begin to recognise manipulative tactics and practise setting healthy boundaries. Conversely, you might better understand other people's points of view and consider what, if anything, you yourself have contributed to the challenging situation.

Maybe you'll conclude that the challenge is not likely to go away, or that its untenable and that it's time to move on. But in such cases, it is you that is making the decision, from a position of strength and acceptance. You're not just running away from a difficult situation that you can't cope with.

Either way, the negative experience becomes a catalyst for developing greater inner strength and emotional resilience. This approach will help you handle future challenges with increased strength and self-assurance.

Connect With Your Inner Wisdom

Listen to messages from your heart, and to your gut instincts, to detect, understand, and deal with psychic attack. This is your inner guidance system, intuitive aspects of yourself that enable you to tune in to your surroundings in ways that go beyond rational thought.

Messages from your heart and gut provide insights into your emotions and desires. They can also tune in to what's going on in your environment. By taking notice of these messages, you can detect subtle shifts in intention and energy before they fully manifest and avoid situations and people, detrimental to your wellbeing.

The gut is often called the second brain because of its evolutionary role in the development of human survival instincts. Put simply, the gut can alert you to potential risks and opportunities.

Our prehistoric ancestors shared their world with dangerous, powerful predators. Early humans often needed to make split second decisions to survive and take advantage of opportunities. As civilisation evolved, other humans became the biggest danger. Today we still have that rapid response capability to assess a situation using subtle cues that are not obvious to the conscious mind.

The gut has its own complex nervous system which can operate independently of the brain and the central nervous system. It also works in concert with both. Neurotransmitters and hormones related to stress and anxiety such as serotonin and cortisol are present in the gut.

Your heart gives you emotional intelligence, resonance with your own values and desires, and empathy with the emotional states of others.

Your heart will tell you if something feels right. You could get a sensation of lightness warmth, excitement, or you might feel joyous, expansive, fulfilled, blissful, at peace. If something isn't right, you may get a tightness in your chest, discomfort, heaviness. Or you might panic, or suddenly feel anxious, sad or drained.

Messages from your gut are more physical and instinctive. Like a knot in your stomach, butterflies, excitement or the sense of being grounded or off planet. Your body processes information quickly and subconsciously by using these sensations.

Like Spider-man's spider sense, this is your inner guidance system telling you that something is wrong. It's nudging you to use your intellect and your other senses to question what you're about to do.

So, for instance, if your heart is telling you that you feel fulfilled that might indicate that you are aligning with your true passions. Persistent anxiety suggests something needs to change or that you're not being true to yourself.

To understand your gut feelings, notice physical reactions say when you're faced with a new decision, experience or social situation. If you feel discomfort that might mean something is not right a feeling of ease might indicate that you're heading in the right direction.

In both cases take a moment to reflect on the feelings and sensations and think about what in this situation, might be triggering these responses. Look for patterns and themes in the messages, gather more information about the situation, think through potential outcomes of what you're doing.

By doing this you can work out whether the messages from your gut and heart are supported by evidence and objective data. Come up with an action plan based on your intuitive insights and rational analysis. Then when you act, see if the results align with your initial feelings, Also check whether things worked out the way you wanted them to do. If necessary, adjust your approach and then listen for further reactions in your gut and your heart, to see if the new approach is working.

Sometimes guidance from your heart and your gut may seem at odds with what you're being told to think and feel about a situation. The contradictory information could be coming from people you know, peers, wider society, the TV, politicians, celebrities, influencers. Never mind about all that; it's your gut, your heart and your intellect that will tell you what's really going on with you and your universe.

Become More Self-Aware

The world is full of information. Information that we can see, hear, smell, taste and feel. But also, as mentioned earlier, there's information out there that you can't locate with your senses. This is why being aware of your thoughts is important. You'll also need to tell the difference between what's coming from inside you and what you're picking up from external sources.

Inner clarity helps you blot out all the noise and discern what's yours and what is not. Psychic attacks are almost always covert assaults, so if you possess this inner clarity, it's easier to defend yourself.

Mindfulness is where you make a deliberate effort to notice what is going on, only in the present moment. Focus on your mind, body and your surroundings and shut everything else out – all distractions. In this state, you take your attention away from past problems and worries about the future. You also notice how thoughts come into your mind and how to let go of them. And become aware of unhealthy or unhelpful thought patterns.

When you do this, you'll have more choice over how to respond to thoughts and feelings and better cope with unhelpful thoughts.

Three Steps Towards Mindful Self Awareness

Observe. Every day, make time to quiet the mind and cultivate inner stillness. A few minutes of centred breathing will do to start - you can add more time as you become more proficient. When you're doing this, thoughts, emotions, or sensations will arise. Observe them with curiosity and compassion and let them drift away.

Notice the sensations that arise in your body as you go about your daily business – when you eat, walk, read, work. Bring your full attention to each moment. Savour each sensory experience and appreciate its richness.

Afterwards, record your thoughts, emotions and experiences in a journal. Write freely, no one will see it but you, so don't worry about spelling, sentence structure, handwriting or constructing a coherent meaning or argument. Forget all that stuff, just let it all pour out.

Reflect. Do you notice any recurring themes? If so, explore them, not with judgement or analytical mindset, but with curiosity and compassion. Notice when you feel negative, say after you've been on social media, or while watching TV or interacting with a certain person or place. This could be an indicator that you are being affected by external energies. Your thoughts may also give you an indication as to whether this is a deliberate psychic attack or if you are just picking things up from your environment.

Set Boundaries. Be aware of situations and people who may exert influence and put your shields up because these people are showing that you have weaknesses in certain areas. It could be your mother-in-law, your boss, your partner or a stranger. Whoever it is, be discerning about the information and viewpoints you allow in. Exercise critical thinking when consuming information and listening to what people say. And notice how external sources of information affect your thoughts emotions and energy. Get to know what is right for you.

Manage Overwhelm and Accept the Flow of Life

Are you easily overwhelmed? Predisposed to resist the natural ebb and flow of life? Problems with either can leave you susceptible to psychic attack. However, if you modify the way you approach life you can develop internal resilience to this.

Prioritise and understand self-care in your relationships so that relationships are healthy, balanced and maintain your happiness as well as those of others. When you don't do this, you may inadvertently attract people who are concerned only with their own selfish needs and send signals to people that only there needs matter, not your own.

Self-care does not mean you're selfish, irrespective of what anyone may have told you. The selfish ones are usually the people who complain about you being selfish. What have you done for me lately! And that's a statement not a question!

Self-care is essential if you want to create relationships based on trust, respect and mutual support. Set healthy boundaries that reflect your own needs desires and make clear, the things that make you feel uncomfortable or disrespected. Communicate your needs honestly and clearly. Be kind to yourself, particularly when you make a mistake, or in times of stress and conflict. In this way you can nurture mutually healthy connections with others.

When you're overwhelmed, your emotional state can become volatile, and you are more likely to use poor coping strategies. As a result, it becomes harder to recover from stress or perceived attacks.

How to Manage Overwhelm. If you are particularly sensitive to your environment and relationships, you will also be more sensitive than most to negative energies and hostile intentions.

When overwhelmed you may misinterpret situations as threats or worry about potential psychic attacks. Mental fatigue can set in and can stop you thinking clearly. You might avoid social interactions or neglect self-care. Ironically, isolating yourself can make you feel more vulnerable and fearful about external threats.

To manage overwhelm, first identify potential triggers and design practices to deal with them. Set realistic expectations of what you can accomplish, and from this prioritise your tasks which you then break down into smaller, more manageable steps.

For many people, overwhelm is a serious issue. If you're susceptible to overwhelm, there will be moments, days, weeks when you will need to take time out for yourself. Talking to a parent, friend or your doctor is all-important here, because you need people who understand this about you.

Accept that Life is Full of Ups and Downs. If you resist the fluctuations in your own life, the lives of others, and the world around you, you'll face a continuous struggle against circumstances that are beyond your control.

Resist the natural flow of life and you'll find yourself in a constant state of tension, as you struggle to make sure things turn out to your liking. You'll also attract negative influences, if you fight the flow of life. Paradoxically, the more you fight, the more you're likely to feel out of control.

You might resist change because you feel vulnerable. However, if you don't accept your own weaknesses or understand that challenges you face are an inevitable part of life, you create a rigid and fragile psychological structure that doesn't cope well with stress.

You might then feel exposed when you encounter negativity and during those moments, have difficulty processing emotions. Unresolved emotions, when they build up, can attract negative energies and people who sense this weakness and seek to capitalise on it.

If, however, you tune into the subtle shifts within yourself, others and the outside world, you can gain deeper insights into what is going on with you. From this, you'll be better able to adapt to whatever comes your way.

By embracing the flow of life, you can see other options when things don't go as planned, or when situations don't work out how you want them to. Accepting that life is about change as well as continuity, makes it easier for you to protect yourself from psychic attack. With a more flexible approach, toxic people and negative energies will find it harder to push you into a corner where you think and feel that there's no way out.

Psychic Protection in Popular Culture

Psychic attack and psychic protection are popular themes in films books and TV shows. These tales and the characters in them tap into our fascination with the supernatural and our desire to explore the unknown. We find it intriguing that the mind can be influenced by unseen forces that we can't fight physically. However, when we see this happening on TV or read about it, deep-rooted fears are exposed. In private moments we might even wonder if such things could happen in our lives, too.

Psychic attack doesn't just happen in fictional realms of fantasy. In more grounded narratives, psychic attack is portrayed as internal struggles, self-empowerment crises and challenges to the limits of human tolerance - concepts everyone can identify with.

Psychic attack and protection are also rooted in culture, history, folklore, mythology, belief and spirituality. These concepts cut across ethics and morals, fears and worries, emotional and mental wellbeing, interpersonal relationships and social dynamics. When you watch, read or hear a story that explores psychic attack and psychic protection, you delve into the very depths of human consciousness. There really is something for everyone in these tales, and you can learn a lot from them.

Take the X-Men comics for instance. In a world of mutants, superheroes and supervillains, powerful telepaths - Jean Grey, Professor X, Emma Frost, Storm and Psylocke often encounter powerful mental threats. They must protect themselves against psychic attacks, mental invasions and manipulation from villains like Mastermind, Mr Sinister and Apocalypse to name three of the worst. Faced with this sort of threat, one technique the X-psychics often use is the psychic shield.

Like a mental firewall, the X-psychics project powerful mental barriers to protect their minds from intruders or to block out invasive thoughts. Magneto, another X-Men adversary, can't do this, so instead he wears an actual helmet to stop people getting inside his head.

You can try this technique out yourself. It's a bit like the Protective Barrier Exercise we looked at earlier. Visualise a powerful shield to create a sense of physical space between you and the unwanted energy. Breathing exercises can also help you control your thoughts and block out external distractions or emotional manipulation.

Vixen is a DC superhero, with a deep spiritual connection to animals, which she uses as a form of psychic protection. She taps into the abilities of the animals she meets, taking on their attributes to protect herself from physical threats and psychic manipulation. She might choose a lion for courage, an owl for wisdom or an elephant for patience and stability. Each animal has its own ways and evoking these qualities can also help us during challenging times.

Like Vixen, focus on a specific animal that represents qualities you need, say protection, inner peace or mental clarity. Doing this can help shield your mind from external pressures, emotional turmoil, or negative energy.

For a more grounded example of psychic protection in popular culture, how about Sayaka Kanamori from the anime 'Keep Your Hands Off Eizouken.' She doesn't have psychic powers, but she does use a form of psychological defence to cope with difficult situations. The processes involved are similar.

Sayaka is good at protecting her personal boundaries, handling stress, external pressures and emotional conflict. She'll use humour to diffuse situations and logic to shield herself from emotional overwhelm, self-doubt and the opinions of others. When under stress, Sayaka creates a mental barrier between her personal feelings and her professional actions. This enables her to stay focused and keep her mind clear of distractions.

From Sayaka you notice how mental and emotional resilience can help you stay focussed on goals. Recognise when you're becoming emotionally overwhelmed, distance yourself from intense emotions, separate your emotional responses from your immediate tasks.

Star Wars

In the Star Wars Universe, the Jedi and the Sith harness the power of 'the Force' to protect themselves psychically. The Force is a mystical energy field that binds the Galaxy together. It possesses a light and dark side and gives those sensitive to it, extraordinary powers.

Both sides use force shields, invisible fields of energy that block or deflect incoming mental and telekinetic attacks. Thought shields protect Force-users' minds from external influence – preventing others from reading their emotions, thoughts and motives.

Using a thought shield requires a strong will, concentration and training. Yoda, for instance, has strong enough mental defences to resist psychic attacks. Luke Skywalker shows his mental toughness by resisting massive psychological pressure to tempt him over to the dark side.

The force can be used to subtly influence the thoughts and actions of others. Or, to directly attack rivals, for instance by triggering fear so that the rival might be more easily controlled.

In the stories, some Force-sensitive individuals use meditation to shield their minds from dark influences. In doing this they strengthen their connection to the force, become more resilient to psychic attack and gain clarity and emotional balance. Others use empathy and telepathy to sense emotions and communicate mentally. The most skilled Force-sensitive individuals can detect disturbances in the force. This heightened awareness enables them to sense threats or hostile intent before they manifest into attacks.

Spider-Man

In the Marvel Comics and films, Spider-Man also has an early warning system called spider-sense that sends him alerts if there is danger around, before the danger happens.

It's a bit like psychic radar. Spider-man can then react to threats before they fully emerge. He can anticipate, avoid and counteract dangerous or threatening situations, without him having to see or hear the danger.

This is useful if you're a fictional superhero who needs to dodge pumpkin bombs thrown by green-suited maniacs from behind skyscrapers. Or detect the hostile intentions of angry alien creatures before they ambush you, creatures which have bonded with resentful rivals and psychotic serial killers.

But you, too, can develop your own intuitive early warning system, to protect you from unseen danger.

Consider past experiences when your instincts guided you or when they failed you. What clues did you pick up on in each situation?

Observe people and environments carefully. Body language, facial expression and other non-verbal clues and subtleties. For instance, some people indicate their discomfort or aggression with crossed arms, tense posture or lack of eye contact.

Listen carefully to what others say particularly tone word choice and underlying emotions. Sarcasm, sudden changes in pitch or tempo or volume can be an indicator of potential threat.

Practice assessing your surroundings, notice who and what is there. Lookout for unusual behaviour. Being aware of your surroundings will help you respond quickly if something goes wrong. Try to understand how conflicts escalate so you can identify potential threats before they become serious

Lord of the Rings

Characters like Frodo, Sam and Boromir attempt to resist the power of the ring and other dark forces, with varying degrees of success.

Frodo shows a great deal of resilience against the ring's psychic assault thanks to his Hobbit simplicity, lack of ambition and because he was pure of heart. Sam's loyalty to Frodo gives him a strong mental defence against the ring's allure. Tom Bombadil is immune to the Ring because of his carefree outlook and deep connexion to nature. In these tales, simplicity and contentment are natural defences against dark influences.

On the other hand, Boromir's desire for power and a belief that he can save his people from the dark forces bring about his downfall, he succumbs to the ring's temptation. It's Galadriel's inner strength, integrity, and foresight that enables her to protect her mind, particularly when she resists the temptation to take the ring from Frodo. Gandalf uses his mental fortitude to protect himself from Saruman's psychological manipulations and dark magic. Sauron can reach into minds and instil fear doubt and corruption.

In Lord of the Rings, characters who possess mental fortitude and humility have a more robust defence against psychic attack. The stories show how mental fortitude creates resilience and how it helps the characters control thoughts and emotions. And how it prevents doubts, insecurities and vulnerabilities from taking hold. Humility keeps certain characters grounded and self-aware, able to recognise their limitations and fallibilities. This prevents arrogance and overconfidence from setting in and decisions being made from ego – traits that psychic attackers can exploit.

Bram Stoker's Dracula

Count Dracula uses psychic and psychological manipulation to control, manipulate, and torment his victims mentally and emotionally. He also uses hypnotic powers to subdue and manipulate people, making them susceptible to his influence and vulnerable to further exploitation.

In this tale, Dracula was a master of instilling fear to weaken his victims. His very presence would create terror and turn people into an emotional wreck. But he was also able to use his charm to persuade people to submit to him voluntarily. He would also target people close to his enemies to create tensions and mistrust in the enemy's life. This can be seen as a form of psychic attack which aims to isolate his enemies and make them more vulnerable.

Like the psychic vampires we encounter in the real world, Dracula would overwhelm his victims with psychic attack before, in his case, draining their blood, not just their energy. It's possible that the sort of people who today we call psychic or energy vampires, could have been the stimulus for stories like Dracula and even for ancient vampire legends. As explained earlier, being around an energy vampire for too long can leave you feeling drained, exhausted and mentally and emotionally. Way back when, it wouldn't take much for a superstitious peasant, a creative storyteller or a religious spin doctor to have connected this sort of effect with a blood sucking acolyte of Beelzebub.

Imagine the scene:

The room was still, the wind whispered through the cracked window. Breath shallow, heart pounding; fear crept towards her like an icy tendril. Thoughts blurred, her mind raced as if something was pressing in, suffocating, inveigling.

A silent command wrapped itself around her mind. Inside her head, a menacing whisper echoed. Her body tensed, her will began to crumble. As she slipped towards darkness; in her minds-eye, a face appeared, blank and still. Cruel lips smiled....

Cue spine-chilling music and audience screams!

They Live!

This is John Carpenter's film about an alien takeover of the world. In the story, the aliens' control everything with subliminal messages that are used to hide their presence and manipulate us into following their orders.

The story takes a twist when a man called Nada finds some special sunglasses through which he can see what is hidden beneath the subliminal messages. Commands like obey, consume and conform are hidden in advertisements, signs, on TV, in newspapers and other everyday objects. Psychically suppressed, people are unable to perceive the true nature of their reality and as such are easily subjugated by the aliens.

Using the sunglasses, Nada can also see that many wealthy and powerful people are, aliens in disguise, invisible to the human eye. The glasses provide mental liberation enabling those who wear them to resist subliminal control and alien influence. Trouble is, no one believes Nada, think he's a fantasist. Until they put on the glasses that is.

In this story, the sunglasses act as a metaphor for our heightened state of consciousness and awareness and represent a person's ability to perceive hidden truths and resist external control.

The story explores the links between consumerism, conformity, media influence, brainwashing, propaganda and covert efforts to control people.

Agatha Christie's Curtain: Poirot's Last Case

In Agatha Christie's last ever Hercule Poirot book, the famous Belgian detective faces an enemy who uses psychological tricks to get people to commit murders. Stephen Norton appears to be an innocuous little man, quite superfluous and ineffective. But this is all a cover.

Norton is actually a highly intelligent, devious individual who has an extraordinary ability to read people's emotions and weaknesses.

Like the Shakespearean character Iago, in Othello, Norton knows exactly what to say and do to influence others to act, without the target even realising that they have been goaded into action.

Norton plants ideas into the minds of his targets. Taking advantage of their frustrations, guilt and anger, he carefully nudges them towards committing murders. Norton's victims believe that they're acting out of their own choice and have no idea that they have been baited into murderous action.

In one scene from the story, Norton provokes Poirot's friend, Captain Hastings, into a fury against Major Allerton. Norton tells Hastings that Allerton, a married man, had been making inappropriate advances towards Hastings' daughter, Judith. Hastings snaps after several days of subtle grooming from Norton, who convinces the captain that Allerton is a scoundrel with low morals.

Norton's true motivation for pitting Hastings against Allerton is revealed later. Allerton had bullied Norton at school. Captain Hastings is on his way up the stairs to Allerton's room to poison the supposed philanderer, when Poirot, who is on to Norton's game, stops his friend from committing murder. Just in time.

Norton is a psychopath, deriving pleasure from the power he holds over others and the chaos that he can create. His superficial charm makes others overlook him, although Poirot suspects him of involvement in five previous murders. With no chance of the man stopping his sinister little games, and Poirot himself, terminally ill with a heart condition, the detective decides to do the one thing he had never done before. He shoots Norton in the head and then arranges things to make it look like suicide. Finally, the manipulator is out manipulated.

Norton's psychological manipulation is a form of psychic attack. He penetrates and influences minds in a way that subtly and powerfully controls thoughts and actions. He gains access to the most vulnerable aspects of his target's psyche and exploits these insecurities. His implanted suggestions resonate with his target's darkest thoughts which are craftily designed to influence the target towards destructive violent and harmful actions - which they believe are a response to their own thoughts. This is a subtle, invisible and chilling form of psychic attack.

Harry Potter and Friends

Harry and his friends use psychic protection to defend themselves against dark magic that targets the mind and the emotions. Without this protection, their enemies can exploit the children's secrets, fears and vulnerabilities. With creatures like dementors around, not to mention Voldemort and his acolytes, it is essential that those on the side of good can guard against despair and fear and resist manipulation. They do this in a few ways.

Legilimency Is a magical ability enabling the user to delve into another's mind and access their thoughts and memories. Voldemort uses this mind reading technique to get information from people and manipulate them.

In Order of the Phoenix, Voldemort infiltrates Harry's mind in his dreams and visions. The 'One Who Shall Not Be Named' hopes to manipulate Harry into retrieving the prophecy from the Department of Mysteries. The visions start off as glimpses into Voldemort's thoughts, but they soon become intrusive and painful and affect Harry's mental and emotional state. Voldemort's dark images of Sirius Black being tortured at the Ministry of Magic further manipulate Harry and lure him into a trap.

Dumbledore and Snape can resist Legilimency by using occlumency. Occlumency is a magical discipline enabling the user to shield their mind from external intrusions and influence. It's particularly important for Snape, a double agent who is pretending to work for Voldemort.

In the Harry Potter stories characters use protective charms to act as barriers against psychic attack. The Protego Charm creates a magical shield to flex hexes and curses. The Fidelius protects a secret by concealing it within the mind of the chosen secret keeper. A Petronas wards off mind-hacking dementors. The Pensieve is a magical object that helps extract and review memories and provide the user with clarity and perspective. Mental clarity is a great protection against psychic attack whereas if you're confused, you're more easily manipulated.

Harry Potter and friends possess considerable internal strength, which enables them to resist dark magic. Willpower, intuition, logical minds, friendship but also a strong sense of self, see the characters through several hairy moments. But in these stories, there's another stronger form of psychic defence. One that provides a deep psychic bond between Harry and his friends and that can shield them from dark forces, better than any other – love.

Love: Essential Psychic Protection

Love is one of the most powerful and transformative forces in human existence. It has the potential to heal, uplift, and protect, but can also function as a deeply rooted psychic shield that guards you from harm. In its various forms - self-love, love for others, and universal love - it offers strength and solace in the face of life's challenges

Self-Love

Without a healthy sense of self-love, it becomes easy to all fall into patterns of negativity, insecurity, and emotional instability. All of which makes you susceptible to psychic attack.

Self-love isn't narcissism or arrogance; it's just respect for yourself, a state of being where you appreciate that you are worthy of care, compassion, and kindness.

With self-love, you have an emotional and mental fortress that shields you from harmful energy - whether that harmful energy comes from others or from inside yourself.

Instead of criticising yourself, telling yourself that you're unworthy or incapable; you nurture and support yourself through life's challenges. Self-loathing, the opposite of self-love, can lead to depression anxiety and a weakened sense of self. Conversely, with self-love you understand your own worth and from this you can develop resilience and reject negative thought patterns.

With self-love you can better manage your feelings. With the greater emotional intelligence it brings, you are less likely to absorb the emotions of others or let people and situations that you encounter erode your peace. Your boundaries will be stronger, you'll less likely feel obliged to others out of fear of upsetting them. You'll also find it easier to distance yourself from toxic people and situations.

Love for Others

Connections with other people can strengthen our mental, emotional and spiritual defences.

What we mean here is genuine love for others, not a desire to please, rescue or possess others. This is something entirely different, usually motivated by insecurity.

Genuine love for others fosters a sense of support, safety and belonging. Relationships built on mutual respect and care can insulate you against the harshness of life, helping you feel safe and empowered.

When you love others, you also allow yourself to be loved. This exchange of positive energy creates a supportive network that shields you from negativity and harm. Supportive partners, friends and family can help you cope emotionally during difficult times. Love for others also nurtures a sense of shared responsibility, which helps when things are challenging.

Loving others creates a positive energetic field around you and your loved ones that can keep negativity away. Empathy and understanding replaces judgement and misunderstanding. In a loving environment, people are more likely to act with kindness, patience, and compassion.

Universal Love

Universal love - love for all beings, regardless of differences - flows from an acceptance of the interconnectedness of all things and an understanding that everyone and everything is part of the same, greater, whole.

Universal love extends to every living thing, transcends personal relationships and serves as a buffer against fear, hatred, and division. It's a constant force that transcends the barriers that appear to divide us.

Embrace universal love and you focus on unity not separation, acceptance rather than judgement. Other people become fellow travellers on the same journey rather than threats or competitors. Even when times are chaotic, you'll be able to remain calm and centered. It's the perfect psychic shield that helps you dissolve feelings of anger, resentment, or fear, and rise above petty conflicts.

Taken together, self-love, love for others, universal love, provide you with the strongest form of psychic protection. Love nurtures, strengthens, and connects. It also underpins all other forms of psychic protection mentioned in this book, making each easier to achieve and more effective.

Each of the three types of love plays its part. Self-love builds inner strength and emotional resilience; love for others gives you a support network that can protect you from negativity; universal love fosters peace and harmony.

Together, they are a protective force that shields your mind, body and spirit from harm, a magnet that will attract joy into your life, and a beacon that helps you can navigate life's challenges with grace, dignity, and peace of mind.

A Final Word

Psychic energy is a powerful tool for human growth.

You really can create a reality in line with your greatest desires by developing awareness of your energy body and using the power of intent. But don't forget that you're mixing with other energies all the time, most often without realising the effect they can have on you. This, in a nutshell, is why you need psychic protection.

I've shared some practices that will help you retain or regain, control over you mind body and spirit, and help you support others do the same. But how well you use these tools and to what extent you are successful in using them to help achieve your goals? That will depend on you.

We live in interesting times. Good luck on your journey!

Printed in Great Britain
by Amazon